The Changing Face of America

A Proud Heritage The Hispanic Library

The Changing Face of America

Hispanic Roots, Hispanic Pride

Deborah Kent

The Child's World

Published in the United States of America by The Child's World®
PO Box 326 • Chanhassen, MN 55317-0326 • 800-599-READ • www.childsworld.com

Acknowledgments

The Childs World®: Mary Berendes, Publishing Director
Editorial Directions, Inc.: E. Russell Primm, Editorial Director; Pam Rosenberg, Project Editor;
Melissa McDaniel, Line Editor; Katie Marsico, Assistant Editor; Matt Messbarger, Editorial
Assistant; Susan Hindman, Copyeditor; Susan Ashley and Sarah E. De Capua, Proofreaders;
Chris Simms and Olivia Nellums, Fact Checkers; Timothy Griffin/IndexServ, Indexer; Cian
Loughlin O'Day and Dawn Friedman, Photo Researchers; Linda S. Koutris, Photo Selector
Creative Spark: Mary Francis and Rob Court, Design and Page Production
Cartography by XNR Productions, Inc.

Photos

Cover: Father and daughter watching a rodeo
Cover photograph: Gabe Palmer/Corbis
Interior photographs: AP/Wide World Photos: 26 (Adam Nadel), 27 (Jose Goitia), 30
(Damian Dovarganes); Art Resource, NY/Donne Bryant: 21; Corbis: 9 (James L. Amos), 19
(Bettmann), 24 (Hugh Beebower), 28 (Dennis Degnan) 29 (Lynsey Addario) 31 (Richard
Berenholtz), 32 (James A. Sugar); Getty Images: 16 (Hulton|Archive), 25 (Time Life
Pictures/Hansel Mieth), 34 (Geoff Hansen); The Granger Collection, New York: 18, 23;
James Leynse/Corbis Saba: 33; Les Stone/Corbis Sygma: 35; North Wind Picture Archives:
7, 8, 10, 11, 12, 13-top and bottom, 15, 17, 20.

Library of Congress Cataloging-in-Publication Data

Cataloging-in-Publication data for this title has been applied for and is available from the
United States Library of Congress.

One	The Northern Frontier	6
Two	Manifest Destiny	14
Three	A Blending of Cultures	22
Four	Rising Voices	28
	Timeline	36
	Glossary	38
	Further Information	39
	Index	40

Chapter One

The Northern Frontier

In 1620, a band of British men, women, and children sailed across the Atlantic Ocean on a ship called the *Mayflower*. On the coast of present-day Massachusetts, they founded the Plymouth Colony. People sometimes think of these colonists as the first European settlers in America.

Indeed, the United States has strong British roots. Massachusetts, where the *Mayflower* landed, was one of 13 British colonies along the eastern coast of North America. The United States was born when these colonies broke away from Great Britain in 1776.

Yet settlers from Spain were living in the present-day United States nearly 100 years before the *Mayflower* arrived at the Massachusetts shore. Spanish settlers had an impact over a vast area of land from Florida to California. For nearly 500 years,

Christopher Columbus and his crew on the Santa Maria *see the "New World" for the first time.*

people of Spanish heritage have helped build the nation we know today.

Spain's influence in the Western Hemisphere began in 1492. That year, Christopher Columbus sailed west from Spain in search of a trade route to India. Columbus was born in Italy, but he sailed under the Spanish flag. By accident, he bumped into the Americas. He claimed the land he found for the Spanish king and queen,

A priest preaches Christianity to Native Americans. Spanish priests traveled with the conquistadores and tried to convert the Indians to the Roman Catholic faith.

Ferdinand and Isabella. In the years that followed, Spain sent a stream of explorers to North and South America.

The Spanish explorers hoped to grow rich by finding gold in these new lands. Everywhere they went, they claimed land for Spain. These adventurers were known as **conquistadores.** The immense territory they claimed was called New Spain. At its height, the Spanish empire included most of Central and South America, Mexico, and much of the present-day United States.

Roman Catholic priests went along with every Spanish exploring party. The priests were eager to **convert** Native Americans to Christianity. While the conquistadors searched for gold, the priests tried to convince the Indians to accept the Roman Catholic faith.

The oldest permanent European settlement in the present-day United States is Saint Augustine, Florida.

Saint Augustine was founded in 1564 by a Spanish sea captain, Pedro Menéndez de Avilés. The Spaniards built a stone fort at Saint Augustine with walls 12 feet (4 meters) thick. The Spaniards never found gold in Florida, but they did set up a chain of mission churches throughout the area.

In the meantime, thousands of miles away, Spanish gold-seekers pushed northward from Mexico. They followed rumors that the Native Americans in what is now called New Mexico had priceless treasures. Though they found no gold, the Spaniards established a series of farming settlements.

In 1598, Don Juan de Oñate founded two villages where the Rio Grande meets the Chama River. The villages were named San Juan and San Gabriel. Santa Fe, the capital of New Mexico, was founded in 1610. The people who settled

The Castillo de San Marcos was built between 1672 and 1695 and served as a Spanish military outpost to protect the city of Saint Augustine in what is now the state of Florida. Today it is a national monument run by the U.S. National Park Service.

People traveled to the city of Santa Fe, New Mexico, in covered wagons. In the early 1600s Santa Fe was a remote frontier town.

these towns were Spanish soldiers and their families. Many of the soldiers had married Native American women during their earlier explorations. Their children were called mestizos, meaning they had mixed Spanish and Indian blood. As time passed, many mestizo settlers married Native Americans they met in New Mexico. The European and Indian peoples became deeply intermingled.

The Spanish villages in New Mexico were extremely isolated. The trail over the mountains and through the desert was so rugged that it took two months to travel from Santa Fe to Chihuahua, the major market town in northern Mexico. The settlers in New Mexico were pioneers living on the remote northern **frontier** of New Spain.

Nearly two centuries after the first Spanish settlers reached New Mexico, New Spain sent settlers to

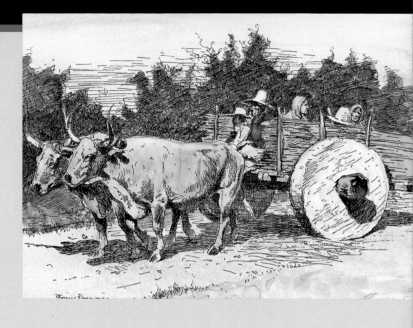

The people of Santa Fe anxiously awaited the trading **caravans** that came from Mexico twice a year. These caravans were long lines of carts pulled by teams of oxen. They were loaded with such goods as copper pots, iron tools, jewelry, perfume, paper, and fine suits and dresses. To the farmers of New Mexico, such items were luxuries. The New Mexicans traded the things they produced on their farms and in their homes for these goods. Among their trade goods were wool blankets, buffalo robes, leather belts, and pine nuts.

Each year, the Mexican city of Chihuahua held a two-week fair. Many families from New Mexico braved the dangers of the trail to attend. Like the traders from the south, they piled their goods onto oxcarts and lumbered over the mountains and across the deserts. The fair in Chihuahua drew up to 50,000 people from all over Mexico. To the New Mexicans, used to the isolation of frontier life, such crowds were almost impossible to believe.

A statue of Father Junípero Serra, the Spanish priest who founded 21 missions in California.

present-day California. In 1769, a priest named Father Junípero Serra founded a mission where San Diego is today. Over the next several years, Father Serra and his followers opened 21 missions in California, from San Diego to present-day San Francisco.

Though New Spain reached from Florida to California, Spanish settlements on the frontier were tiny and scattered. In 1800, the biggest city on the northern frontier was Santa Fe, with about 2,500 people. Some 6,000 people of Spanish descent lived in California, about 30,000 lived in New Mexico, and another 4,000 to 5,000 were sprinkled across Arizona, Texas, and the American Southeast. As time passed, the settlers felt less and less connected to Mexico, which was far to the south. Spain, the mother country, was impossibly far away. The frontier settlers were survivors, and they carved out a new way of life on their own.

Each of the California missions was a farming village with a church at its center. Native Americans lived at the mission in huts made of stone or adobe, a kind of brick. They raised corn and herded sheep, cattle, and horses. Church bells called them to services early each morning.

Life at the missions was not the kind of life that the Native Americans were used to. The priests enforced strict rules. Sometimes families were split up. Many of the Native Americans who lived on the missions did not want to be there. The Spanish priests believed that they were saving the souls of the Indians by forcing them to live on the missions and converting them to Christianity.

Chapter Two

Manifest Destiny

On an autumn morning in 1821, church bells pealed and cannons roared in Santa Fe. After 11 years of fighting, Mexico had won its independence from Spain. All across the northern frontier, people celebrated the news. They were now citizens of a new nation, the Republic of Mexico.

Spain had not allowed its colonists to trade with their neighbors in the United States. Mexico, however, permitted trade with the Americans. In 1821, a Missouri businessman named William Becknell brought wagonloads of American products to Santa Fe. The New Mexicans were eager customers. Becknell returned the following year with an entire wagon train of goods. People flocked to the town square to marvel at Becknell's wares—cloth, nails, paper, glass, shoes, toys, clocks, and pots and pans. Becknell made a

Covered wagons traveled the Santa Fe Trail from Independence, Missouri, to Santa Fe, New Mexico, a distance of 800 miles (1,287 km).

small fortune. Soon other merchants were tramping a path to Santa Fe. The Santa Fe Trail, winding its way 800 miles (1,287 kilometers) from Independence, Missouri, to Santa Fe, became an American legend.

Ever since the United States won its independence from Great Britain, Americans had been looking westward. In 1803, the United States bought almost 900,000 square miles (2,331,000 square km) of land west of the Mississippi River from France in the Louisiana Purchase.

Three years later, American army officer Zebulon Pike ventured into Mexico's northern frontier. He wrote a glowing account of the area's fertile soil and beautiful land. After Pike's visit, American fur trappers trekked into the western mountains. The trappers were loners who caught beavers, mink, foxes, and other animals and sold their valuable pelts.

Land-hungry farmers followed Pike and the trappers. They staked claims in thinly populated frontier regions,

U.S. Army officer Zebulon Pike led an expedition to explore Mexico's northern frontier in 1806.

American citizens flocked to Texas to ranch and farm on its endless grasslands. By the 1830s, Anglos living in Texas outnumbered the Mexicans living there by about four to one.

especially the area known as Texas. They raised herds of cattle on Texas's endless grasslands. By 1831, about 30,000 U.S. citizens lived in Texas, compared with only 7,000 Mexicans. The Mexicans referred to these immigrants from the United States as **Anglos.**

Anglo and Mexican cultures were very different. English was the native language of the Anglos, while the Mexicans spoke Spanish. Mexico was a strongly Roman Catholic country, while most of the Anglos were Protestants. Another difference between the two cultures was their attitude toward slavery. To most whites in the southern United States, African-American slavery was an accepted part of life. Slavery was illegal in Mexico.

Slaves work on a cotton plantation. Many Americans brought their slaves with them when they settled in Texas, even though slavery was illegal in Mexico.

Ignoring Mexican laws, Anglos brought their slaves along with them when they settled in Texas.

In the first half of the 19th century, many Americans believed that their country should stretch from the Atlantic to the Pacific Oceans. They believed that God intended the United States to control and tame this vast territory. The idea that the United States should reach from ocean to ocean was called manifest destiny. Statesmen, journalists, and military leaders championed this idea. In order to fulfill its manifest destiny, the United States would have to take possession of Mexico's northern frontier.

In 1836, the Anglos in Texas rebelled against Mexico and formed their own country, the Republic of Texas. Texas was nicknamed the Lone Star Republic because it had a single star on its flag. Ten years later, the United States launched a war against Mexico. The Mexican-American War lasted for two years. The Mexicans fought bravely, but they were overpowered by the U.S. forces. Mexico did not have the strength to hold its northern lands. The treaty of 1848 gave the United States the present-day states of

James K. Polk was president of the United States during the Mexican War. During his presidency, the United States increased greatly in size.

General Winfield Scott leads the U.S. Army into Mexico City during the Mexican War.

New Mexico, Arizona, and California, as well as parts of Nevada, Utah, Colorado, and Oklahoma. In addition, the Lone Star Republic agreed to become part of the United States.

Americans celebrated their victory. As they had hoped, their nation now stretched from coast to coast across the North American continent. But for the Mexican people who lived in the conquered territory, the treaty of 1848 spelled an uncertain future.

Every year, thousands of visitors walk through the gardens and courtyards of the Alamo, a restored Spanish mission in San Antonio, Texas. The Alamo is a quiet retreat from the busy streets all around it. It is hard to believe that the Alamo of today was once the scene of a bloody battle.

In the winter of 1836, Anglo Texans decided to break away from Mexico. Mexico sent an armed force to end the rebellion. A small group of Texans tried to defend the Alamo against Mexican General Antonio López de Santa Anna. Though they were vastly outnumbered, the Texans held the Alamo for 13 days. At last they ran out of ammunition, and the Mexicans swept into the mission fort. Nearly all of the Texans were killed, including the famous frontiersman Davy Crockett. Ten years later, in the Mexican-American War, U.S. troops rushed into battle with the cry, "Remember the Alamo!"

Chapter Three

A Blending of Cultures

A few months after the end of the Mexican-American War, a ranch foreman found specks of gold in a stream near Sutter's Mill, California. Thousands of Anglos poured into California hoping to strike it rich. New towns popped up overnight. Stores, taverns, and Protestant churches lined the streets of these towns. Anglo culture seemed to be taking over the land of missions and ranches.

In Texas, New Mexico, and Arizona, the Anglo population grew steadily. Wherever they came together, Anglo and Mexican cultures influenced one another. People of Mexican heritage learned English and sent their children to American-style schools. Anglos developed a taste for tacos, chiles, beans, and other Mexican foods. They built their houses in the traditional Mexican style, using brick and stone instead of wood.

Prospectors pan for gold in the foothills of the Sierra Nevada mountain range. The gold rush brought many Anglo settlers into California.

Like homes in Mexico, many houses in the Southwest had enclosed courtyards or patios. Hispanic heritage was also reflected in the names chosen for cities and towns across the Southwest. San Antonio, Texas; Santa Fe, New Mexico; and Los Angeles, California, were named by their Spanish founders. Other California cities such as San Diego, Santa Barbara, and San Jose bear the names of early missions.

Dozens of Spanish words found their way into the English language. The word *lariat* comes from the Spanish words *la reata,* meaning "the rope." The Spanish word *corral,* referring to a fenced-in pen, became an English word. The word *savvy,* meaning "clever" or "smart," comes from the Spanish word *saber,* "to know."

By 1898, little remained of the vast empire called New Spain. Through a series of wars, Spain had lost nearly all of its colonies. It held only two small islands in the Americas—Cuba and Puerto Rico. The United States was determined to drive Spain out of the Western Hemisphere forever. The Spanish-American

A rancher uses a lariat to try to lasso a horse. Lariat *is an English word that comes from the Spanish* la reata, *which means "the rope."*

War resulted in independence for Cuba. The island of Puerto Rico became a United States possession.

The territory that the United States had acquired in the Mexican-American War was immense and thinly populated. Puerto Rico, on the other hand, was a small, crowded island. In 1898, it was home to more than a million people, most of them poor and uneducated. At first, U.S. companies ran sugar and coffee **plantations** on the island. Later in the 20th century, American companies in Puerto Rico began turning out chemicals, plastics, and many other products. Yet the Anglo population on the island remained small. Puerto Rico kept its own culture and way of life.

The Jones Act of 1917 granted U.S. citizenship to the people of Puerto Rico. As citizens, Puerto Ricans could move freely to and from the United

A man works on a Puerto Rican sugar cane plantation.

States. In the 1920s, Puerto Ricans began to settle in New York and other cities on the Atlantic coast. Like other immigrants before them, they took low-paying jobs in factories. They worked to build a better life for their children and grandchildren. During the 1950s, Puerto Rican immigration to the United States swelled to a flood. The Puerto Ricans led a new wave of Spanish-speaking immigrants who would transform the United States.

Puerto Ricans in New York City celebrate their heritage during the annual Puerto Rican Day Parade.

In 1960, a dictator named Fidel
Castro seized control of the
island nation of Cuba. Castro's
government promised to take
money and property from the
rich and give it to the poor.
Thousands of wealthy Cubans
fled the island, fearing for their
lives. Leaving their worldly goods behind, they found
refuge in the United States. Many of these Cubans were
well educated. In the United States, they became success-
ful as doctors, teachers, and business managers.

For the most part, Castro failed to deliver what he
had promised to the Cuban people. Cubans were not
allowed to speak out against their government. They
were not even permitted to leave the country. Many
Cubans fled in secret. They braved the ocean in tiny
boats, hoping to get to the United States. If they
survived and reached the coast of Florida, they asked
the U.S. government to protect them. Since the United
States opposed Castro, it welcomed people who fled
from Cuba. Today, more than a million people of Cuban
descent live in the United States.

Chapter Four

Rising Voices

These twin sisters are just two of the many people of Latino heritage who live in the United States.

Every 10 years, the U.S. government conducts a nationwide **census.** The census tells us a great deal about who we are, where we live, and what we do.

The 1990 and 2000 census figures show a startling increase in the Latino population of the United States. The term Latino refers to people who trace their roots to Mexico, Central America, South America, or Spanish-speaking parts of the Caribbean. In 1990, about 8 percent of the people in the United States were Latinos. In 2000, Latinos made up more than 12 percent of the U.S. population. About 32 percent, or nearly one-third, of the people in California claimed Latino heritage in 2000. Latinos are the fastest-growing population group in California.

A group of elementary school students gathers in Sacramento, California. Nearly one out of three people in California claims Latino heritage.

Many people believe that California is leading a national trend. Waves of immigrants from Puerto Rico and Latin America are pouring into cities across the country, from Miami, Florida, to Seattle, Washington. The United States has growing communities of people from nearly every Latin American nation. The largest group of newcomers hails from Mexico. Sizable numbers also come from the Dominican Republic,

A man reads a Spanish-language newspaper in Los Angeles, California.

Cuba, Guatemala, El Salvador, and Colombia. Each of these Latin American nations has its own history, music, food, and customs. Latino immigrants bring a host of traditions to their adopted land.

Latinos are having a powerful impact on U.S. culture. Most cities now have Spanish-language newspapers and radio and TV stations. Many supermarkets stock such foods as tortillas, chili peppers, and plantains (banana-like fruit used in many Puerto Rican and Cuban dishes). Popular songs blend English and Spanish lyrics. Along the border between the United States and Mexico, millions of people speak Spanglish, a mix of the two languages.

Many Latin American nations are poor places where people have little chance to get ahead. To people from Mexico and other Latin American countries, the United States seems to offer opportunity. By working and

The following American cities have the highest Latino populations, according to the 2000 census:

New York, New York:	2,160,554
Los Angeles, California:	1,719,073
Chicago, Illinois:	753,644
Houston, Texas:	730,865
San Antonio, Texas:	671,394
Phoenix, Arizona:	449,972

studying hard in the United States, Latinos hope to improve their lives.

Even in the United States, however, life for Latinos can be difficult and even cruel. Millions of Latinos work as **migrant** farmhands. They move from season to season as the crops ripen. They might pick peaches in Texas, then harvest grapes in California, and next

Migrant workers harvest grapes in California. Millions of Latinos work as migrant farmhands, traveling from farm to farm looking for work.

Many Latinos confront the challenges of poverty on a daily basis, often living in run-down apartments in poor, dangerous neighborhoods.

head north to pack apples in Washington. On most farms, the workers live in tiny, poorly built houses. They barely earn enough money to buy food and clothing. Children change schools every few months and fall farther and farther behind their classmates. In the cities, too, Latinos face painful challenges. Often they must take the dirtiest, lowest-paying jobs available. The only apartments they can afford are in the

César Chávez was a migrant farm worker who organized his fellow laborers into unions that fought for better working conditions. In 1994, one year after he died, he was awarded the Presidential Medal of Freedom for his tireless support of poor, working people.

most rundown sections of town. Gangs and drugs are serious problems.

But change may be coming. Latinos are rising as a political force. Latino men and women have been elected to city councils and state legislatures across the country. Some have become members of the U.S. Congress. They work on issues of special concern to the Latino community and on issues important to all Americans.

Politicians and newscasters sometimes speak of Latinos as "a new voice" rising in the United States. Yet people of Hispanic heritage have been part of the nation from the very beginning. They were here long before British people stepped off the *Mayflower* onto the Massachusetts shore.

Many Latinos enter the United States legally, having gotten the immigration papers that the U.S. government requires. Yet the proper papers can be difficult or even impossible to obtain. Thousands of immigrants without papers come into the country illegally every year. Desperate to enter the United States, they slip across the border from Mexico. Once in the United States, they live in constant fear of being discovered. They can be **deported** back to their

home country or held in special prisons. Sometimes they are mistreated by their employers. Because they are in the United States without the proper papers, illegal immigrants are usually afraid to complain about mistreatment.

1492: Christopher Columbus sails west from Spain seeking a new route to the Indies and finds himself in the Americas, continents previously unknown to the Spanish.

1564: Spaniards establish Saint Augustine, Florida, the oldest city in the present-day United States.

1598: Don Juan de Oñate founds two villages in present-day New Mexico.

1610: Settlers from New Spain found Santa Fe, New Mexico.

1620: The *Mayflower* lands on the coast of Massachusetts.

1672–1695: The Castillo de San Marcos is built.

1769: Father Junípero Serra starts a mission at present-day San Diego, California.

1800: Santa Fe is the largest city in Mexico's northern frontier.

1803: The United States buys almost 900,000 square miles (2,331,000 sq km) of land from France in the Louisiana Purchase.

1806: Zebulon Pike explores Mexico's northern frontier.

1821: Mexico wins its independence from Spain. William Becknell opens the Santa Fe Trail from Missouri to New Mexico.

1831: About 30,000 U.S. Citizens live in Texas, compared with only 7,000 Mexicans.

1836: Anglos in Texas rebel against Mexico and start a new country, nicknamed the Lone Star Republic.

1848: The United States gains Mexico's huge northern frontier as a result of the Mexican-American War. Gold is discovered in California and many Anglo settlers move there to seek their fortunes.

1898: The United States seizes Puerto Rico in the Spanish-American War.

1917: The Jones Act grants U.S. citizenship to the people of Puerto Rico.

1920s: Puerto Ricans begin to settle in New York and other cities on the Atlantic Coast.

1950s: Puerto Rican immigration to the U.S. mainland swells to a flood.

1960: Fidel Castro seizes control of Cuba. Cubans begin fleeing to the United States.

1994: César Chávez is awarded the Presidential Medal of Freedom for his work on behalf of poor, working people.

2000: Census figures show that one-third of all Californians are Latinos.

Glossary

Anglos (ANG-glos) Anglos are non-Hispanic people of European descent. Mexicans referred to U.S. citizens living in Texas as Anglos.

caravans (KARE-uh-vanz) Caravans are large groups traveling together through the desert. Oxcart caravans brought goods from Mexico to the people living on the northern frontier of New Spain.

census (SEN-suhss) A census is an official count of the number of people living somewhere. The U.S. Census in 2000 showed that about one-third of Californians are Latinos.

conquistadores (kon-KEES-tuh-dorz) Conquistadores are conquerors. Spanish conquistadores conquered the Native Americans of Mexico and Peru in the 16th century.

convert (kuhn-VURT) To convert someone is to change that person's beliefs. Priests who traveled with Spanish explorers wanted to convert Native Americans to Christianity.

deported (di-PORE-ted) To be deported is to be forced to leave the country. Illegal immigrants can be deported if they are caught.

frontier (fruhn-TIHR) A frontier is the farthest edge of a settled region. Texas, New Mexico, and California were parts of the northern frontier of New Spain.

migrant (MYE-gruhnt) A migrant is someone who moves from place to place for work. Many migrant farmworkers come from Mexico.

plantations (plan-TAY-shuhnz) Plantations are large farms that raise cotton, tobacco, sugarcane, or coffee. U.S. companies started coffee and sugar plantations in Puerto Rico.

Books

Ancona, George. *Barrio: Jose's Neighborhood.* New York: Harcourt Brace, 1998.

Mora, Pat. *A Library for Juana.* New York: Alfred A. Knopf, 2002.

Parker, Lewis K. *Why Mexican Immigrants Came to America.* New York: PowerKids Press, 2003.

Soto, Gary. *Snapshots from the Wedding.* New York: Putnam, 1997.

Web Sites

Visit our Web page for lots of links about the changing face of America:
http://www.childsworld.com/links.html

Note to parents, teachers, and librarians: We routinely check our Web links to make sure they're safe, active sites—so encourage your readers to check them out!

About the Author

Deborah Kent grew up in Little Falls, New Jersey, and received her bachelor's degree from Oberlin College. She earned a master's degree from Smith College School for Social Work and worked as a social worker before becoming a full-time writer. She is the author of 18 young-adult novels and more than 50 nonfiction titles for children. She lives in Chicago with her husband, children's author R. Conrad Stein, and their daughter, Janna.

Index

Alamo, 21, *21*
Anglos, 17–18, *17,* 22, 23

Becknell, William, 14–15

Castillo de San Marcos, *9*
Castro, Fidel, 27, *27*
census, 28
Chávez, César, *34*
Columbus, Christopher, 7–8, *7*
conquistadores, 8
Cuba, 24–25, 27
culture, 30

deportation, 35

farming, 9, 11, 13, *18,* 25, *25,* 32–33, *32*
Ferdinand, king of Spain, 7–8
fur trade, 16

gold, 8, 9, 22, *23*
Great Britain, 6

homes, 22–23

immigrants, 26, *26,* 27, 29–30, 35, *35*
Isabella, queen of Spain, 7–8

Jones Act (1917), 25

Latinos, 28–29, *28, 29,* 31, 33–34, *33*
Louisiana Purchase, 15

manifest destiny, 19
Menéndez de Avilés, Pedro, 9

mestizos, 10
Mexican-American War, 19, *20,* 21
Mexico, 10, 11, 14, 16, 17, 19, *20,* 21, 29, 35
migrant workers, 32–33, *32*
missions, 9, 12, 13, *13,* 21, 23

Native Americans, 8, *8,* 10, 13
New Spain, 8, 12, 24

de Oñate, Don Juan, 9

Pike, Zebulon, 16, *16*
plantations, *18,* 25, *25*
Polk, James K., *19*
population, 28–29, *28, 29,* 31
Puerto Rican Day Parade, *26*
Puerto Rico, 24–26, *25*

Republic of Texas, 19
Roman Catholicism, 8, *8,* 9, 12, *13,* 13, 17

Saint Augustine, Florida, 8–9, *9*
Santa Anna, Antonio López de, 21
Santa Fe, New Mexico, 9, *10,* 14, 15
Santa Fe Trail, 15, *15*
Serra, Fr. Junípero, 12, *12*
settlers, 6–7, 10–11, 12, *23*
slavery, 17–18, *18*
Spain, 6, 7, 8, 14, 24
Spanish language, 23–24, *24,* 30, *30*
Spanish-American War, 24–25

Texas, 17, *17,* 18, 19
trade caravans, 11, *11*